Making Treasures While Making Do

Documentation
of a
Quilting Legacy

By

Agnes M. Pool

Copyright © 2013

All rights reserved

Published by:
Agnes M. Pool
306 North Deborah Drive
Columbiana, Alabama 35051

ISBN-13 978-0615888996:
ISBN: 0615888992

No part of this publication may be reproduced or transmitted in any form or by any means, electronic or mechanical, including photocopy, recording, or any information storage and retrieval system, without permission in writing from the publisher/author.

Dedication

This book is dedicated to my mother, Nettie Vonzelle Juzan Moore, who taught me to sew and who shared her talents and love of quilting; to my maternal aunt, Mildred Alberta (Bert) Juzan Pettus for sharing the memories of her early years of life in Shelby, Alabama; but especially to my daughter, Sherry Tidwell, for saying: "Mother, you can do this."

Acknowledgments

I would like to thank the following people and organizations for their help in making this book become a reality.

★ My family members who generously shared their legacy quilts: Aunt Mildred Juzan Pettus; cousins: Ann Klecak, Earlene Moore, Jack Moore, Tom Moore, Johnny Moore, Marvin E. Carden, Richard N. Carden; and my sister, Vera Dean Moore Benson.

★ Sarah Atchison for her fine hand quilting and her friendship.

★ Lura Campbell for her talents with Long Arm Quilting.

★ Andrea Bliss for photographing the quilts and for her patience.

★ Fran Sharpe for proofing the written words and for her encouragement.

★ Catherine Moore Brown for helping with the patterns in Excel.

★ Retta Authier for being my sounding board and most always agreeing with me.

★ Shelby Iron Works Park and Museum Members for the use of their facility.

★ J. W. Ross for help with the specs of transferring data to online. He is a computer geek!

Introduction

When I started this project I had no idea that a documentation of family quilts could become so inclusive and consuming! I am up at midnight working on ideas and inserting photos into pages, researching patterns, comparing fabric colors and prints. Oh, but what a wealth of learning!

Because I have been quilting most of my life, I believed I knew a lot about quilting. No! Playing under the quilting frames when young did teach me some things about my mother and my aunts, but not much about quilting. Just because I had made three nine patch quilts by the time I married at 18, did not mean I knew much about quilting. The sewing classes completed over the years did gain me experience and aided with sewing on my quilts. The quilting classes and quilt shows attended have added numerous techniques to my quilting skills.

The Documentation Project of my late maternal aunt's legacy of quilts has increased my learning curve by miles! Of course, we all appreciated my Aunt Natie's (Na-tie) quilts. After her death in 2006, at age 97, we scrambled to make sure at least one of her quilts came our way. She was a QUILTER. This documentation project of her quilts has made me aware of just what it does take to make a quilter!

In the 80 years span of her quilt making, she made mathematical decisions that turned into aesthetically pleasing works of art. She had an eye for color and she used it boldly. She dared to make quilts from patterns never seen before; all without the aid of rotary cutters, cutting mats, magazines filled with all type patterns and techniques, all the modern sewing tools and machines, ---and without the aid of a tutorial on YouTube! Things I depend on every day.

The search for her quilts has given me a greater understanding of the efforts she made to create 'pleasing to her eye' bed covers that served their purpose of keeping her family warm and comfortable. She saved and used scraps and pieces of fabrics for years. Most quilters from her time period did the same, but because her quilts have been saved and preserved, they can now be compared. Some of the same fabrics in her 1920's quilts were found in her 1960's quilts. I have a greater appreciation of my yards of fabric in my stash because I see that she had limited amounts of fabric yet made patchwork squares from those amounts that were appropriate interpretations of patterns.

I have read that it is rare to be able to compare and document more than one or two quilts from one quiltmaker or family. My family must be an exception. Natie Juzan left a legacy of some thirty quilts. These quilts, even though not one of them have been entered in a contest or ever won an award, have been lovingly cherished and preserved by her family.

On the pages that follow, you will find my Aunt Natie's quilting story, family photos and photographs and information of some of her vintage quilts. None of her quilts were included in the Alabama Quilt Documentation Project. Instructions for my versions of several of the quilts are included along with photos and patterns. Although Natie made her quilts the traditional way, I have taken shortcuts and used todays methods and tools to create a sampling of a few of the traditional patterns she used.

I have learned a great deal about quilting and making quilts from this documentation project. The research into pattern sources and names has been an education in itself. My fabric and pattern library has increased to the point of needing another bookcase.

The simple process of documenting our quilts is as important today as is documenting our families quilting legacies. Sew a label on your completed quilt. Fill out a personal documentation form and store with your important papers for future generations.

CONTENTS

Title Page	iii
Copyright	iv
Dedication	v
Acknowledgments	vi
Introduction	vii
Contents	ix

Chapter One — 1
Documenting the Quilts
Inspiration Fan Quilt

Chapter Two — 7
Story of Quiltmaker and Photos
Robbing Peter to Pay Paul Quilt
Trip Around the World Lap Quilt

Chapter Three — 39
Gathering and Hanging the Quilts
Appliqued Butterfly Baby Quilt
Dresden Plate Table Runner

Chapter Four — 49
Planning an Exhibition
Tree of Life Wall Hanging
Spider Web Strip Star

Chapter Five — 59
Lessons Learned
Hosanna

References	62
About Author	63

Chapter One

Documenting the Quilts

Quilt documentation is the process of gathering and preserving information for the use of future researchers. Researchers are beginning to realize the value of documenting family quilts.

For a family documentation project the published guidelines have to be modified. My maternal aunt had no children; therefore the quilts were given to family members. Some family members live a distance away, so planning a Documentation Day turned into several days.

Telephone rates were high due to the many calls concerning the location of the quilts. Cousins from Florida brought four quilts for the first foray into the process. We set up folding tables and hung the quilts on the wall in the garage, made photos with a digital camera and lovingly examined, measured and recorded our findings of each one. That first session took four hours for four quilts.

A cousin from West Alabama brought over the next quilts. He brought bags of quilts. The snag with this stack of quilts was that his mother had died within the last year and he did not know which quilts our aunt had made and which his mother had made. We documented several that we had questions about.

With experience of the process now, and the purchase of a quilt display rod and learning to sew quilt sleeves, the quilts brought again by cousins from West Alabama were documented in less time. We called in our 92-year-old aunt who resides in Talladega County, to help with identification of those we had questions about. This session netted 15 more quilts documented.

My sister helped me document five from our immediate family members. Family quilt documenting, I have found, cannot be concluded in one or two sessions. There are several quilts made by my Aunt that have not been documented as of yet— four or five.

The Inspirational Quilt

This *Fanny's Fan* Quilt made circa 1960, was hand pieced and hand quilted by Lillian Natie Juzan. 72" x 90" with 110 on-point 7" x 7" blocks. Owner: Dean Benson, niece of maker.

Natie made three fan patterned quilts that have been documented. This is by far the most striking. The on-point setting, seven fan blades and the use of plaids and checks sets this one apart. It is almost 3D. The placement of dark and light blades gives it the look of art Deco. *Grandmother's Fan* patterns usually have six or eight multi-colored blades. This pattern is an adaptation of an 1870s *Fanny's Fan* pattern. The black base anchors the blades, the wide blue print border contains the fans, and the red chambray lining turned to the front as a binding adds to the framing of the colorful fans. The quilting pattern is two inch parallel lines.

Fans All Ways Quilt

1930s reproduction fabrics, machine paper pieced, hand appliqued and hand quilted, these seven-inch squares have seven fan blades with the black base, inspired by the ones made by my Aunt Natie Juzan.

36" x 40"   Agnes Pool, June 2012

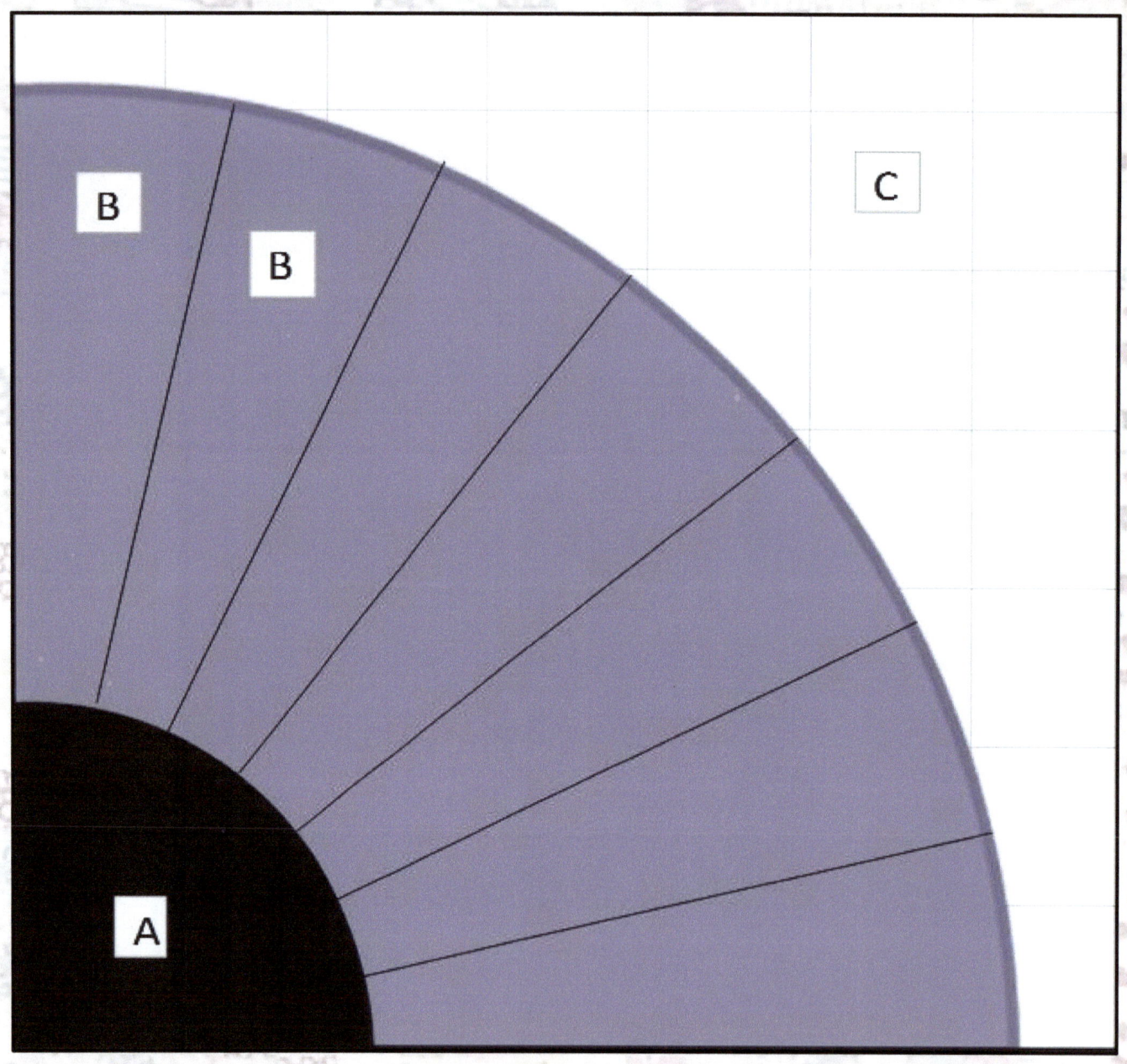

7" Fan Block for *36" x 40" FANS ALL WAYS*

Copy the sheet to use as a foundation for paper piecing the fan blades.

Applique A and C to pieced blades to complete the block.

For piecing the entire block, be sure to add ¼ inch to A, B, and C for seam allowances

Fabric Requirements

A—Fat Quarter of Solid Fabric

B—1 Charm Pack of Print Fabric

B—1 Charm Pack of Coordinating Solid

C—3 Yards for Background and Backing

Borders and Binding—1 Yard Coordinating Fabric

Batting—40" x 45"

Yardage is based on 40" wide.

Cutting Directions

Cut **21** - 7" Squares from background fabric, **13** for Fan Squares and **2** Setting Squares.

Cut the **6** squares in half on the diagonal for filling in setting squares on point.

From Fat Quarter Solid Fabric Cut **13** of Pattern A.

Cut **4** - 4 ½" pieces WOF from Coordinating Print for Borders

Cut **5** - 2 ½" pieces WOF from coordinating fabric for Binding

Sewing the quilt

Make **13** Fan Squares

Set together in diagonal rows, adding setting pieces, according to the illustration or according to your fancy.

Sew side borders then top and bottom borders.

Layer and Quilt as desired.

Sew Binding strips together; fold and press wrong sides, finish the edges with double-fold binding.

Be sure to add your label!

Chapter Two

Portrait of a Quilter

Lillian Natie Juzan

June 22, 1909 – September 27, 2006

Born the oldest of seven children to John William Juzan and Florence Belle Baldwin Juzan, Natie quilted many quilts in her long life. Belle, an accomplished seamstress, by necessity of the times in rural Alabama, taught Natie sewing. By the time Woodrow Wilson had signed the Armistice Agreement and World War I had ended, Natie had already made her first quilt. She was nine years old.

John Juzan family in the spring of 1926, Shelby Springs, Shelby County, Alabama. Natie (top left) attended Shelby Springs School. She completed eighth grade.

Robbing Peter to Pay Paul

The search for Natie's quilts reached back in time to the early 1900's. She would have been in her teens when this quilt was made.

Owner: nephew, Marvin E. Carden

This quilt, circa 1925, was from an earlier pioneer pattern, **Robbing Peter to Pay Paul**. The quilt is a smaller quilt, 60″ x 72″. Pattern names include: "Bay Leaf", "Orange Peel" and "Pin Cushion."

Mildred, one of her younger sisters, remembers her mother fussing at Natie about the size of the applique stitches on the yellow centers. Belle had her re-do several!

This ***Trip Around the World*** quilt Natie pieced and quilted, circa 1925. The size is 60" x 75" and the fabrics are indicative of the 1920s pastels. The blue and lavender background fabrics used in the *Robbing Peter to Pay Paul* quilt were used to make some of the 2 ½ inch squares in this quilt. The double pinks and softer colored calicos were fabrics from this time period. Some stabilization has been necessary for this well-worn quilt.

The family had several "one man iron beds or three quarter beds" and it is supposed that the smaller quilts were for these beds. The size of the quilts increased by the early 1950s.

These early quilts, even though showing years of wear and washings, have been lovingly kept by the youngest of Natie's sisters, Belle Marie. After the death of my grandparents and uncle, Natie gave up the house in the country and Belle Marie asked for the old quilts. Her children have them now as she died in 2011.

The lighter fabrics in the circa 1940 *Windmill/Kaleidoscope* quilt are some of the same fabrics in the *Trip Around the World*. Natie did parallel line quilting two inches apart on several of her quilts. The majority of the quilts documented have parallel lines quilting.

Kaleidoscope Circa 1940   Owner: niece, Dean Benson

Detail

The border fabric in this *Caesar's Crown* quilt is the same fabric used in the *New Jersey* strip quilt. Some of the plaid fabrics in 1937 *Southern Bell* were used in both. There is another quilt made by this same pattern, but is too fragile and worn to handle.

Needle turned applique was used in the centers of these pieced squares and the back has a light colored print.

Caesar's Crown   Circa 1945   66" x 80"
Hand pieced and hand quilted by Natie Juzan
Owner: nephew, Marvin E. Carden

Bars Quilt 1948

The fabric in this quilt when purchased was on rolls four inches wide --- some type mill end. The plaid fabric was cut on the diagonal. Natie cut and pieced the four-inch strips, made 12-inch squares and set them together as blocks to make the horizontal bars. The blocks are evident in the quilting lines on the back of the *Bars* quilt.

Bars by Natie Juzan 68″ x 74″
Owner: Marvin E. Carden, nephew

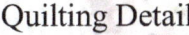

Quilting Detail

There were two quilts made from this pattern that have been documented. This one was made first. The plaid fabrics from the 1930s were used in this *New Jersey Strip* quilt pattern.

New Jersey Strip Quilt 64″ x 80″   1950
Hand pieced and hand quilted by Natie Juzan
Owner: niece, Dean Benson

The detail close-up shows plaid fabrics that were used in several others. The shirting fabric dates from the 1900s.

Checks and stripes---lots of stripes make this fan unique. Using the straight set for this *Grandmother's Fan*, she turned the fans to the left, opposite of the traditional setting. Natie used green patterned stripes for the setting/background squares and a darker green stripe for the base of the fans. The green patterned stripes were used in the *Robbing Peter to Pay Paul* quilt over 40 years before. Again the use of light and dark fabrics gives a bold look to this quilt. The green small print border and purple chambray back turned to the front for the binding was an even bolder use of fabric.

Grandmother's Fan   Circa 1960   72" x 84"
Owner: Mildred Juzan Pettus, sister

This close-up of the 7 x 7 inch squares show stripes, plaids, novelty prints, calicos and solids, all turned to the left. Some of the fabrics were used in the *Fanny's Fan* quilt.

This quilt was made for Natie's brother who lived in a nursing home for several years before his death. Well-washed and faded, the quilt still has distinctive lines. Scraps of all colors and sizes set on point were put to good use in this **Hour Glass** scrap quilt. The back is turned to the front as a binding and has a machine zigzag hem; one of three quilts with machine stitching documented.

Hour Glass   Circa 1960, Owner: niece, Dean Benson

Close-up detail of square and name on the back required by nursing home facility.

Appliqued and embroidered quilts were the focus of Natie's quilts from the 1950s through the 1970s. *Dresden Plate, Dutch Dolls, Four Tulips and Butterflies,* all with the black floss that was popular after the 1920s.

Without sashing or frames, these spirals seem to float on the white background.
Notice the plaids in the **Dresden Plate** squares, the same as the 1937 *Southern Bell*.
Her scrap bag runneth over!

Detail of the square shows the accuracy and neatness of her workmanship.

Dresden Plate 76" x 90" Circa 1960 Owner: niece, Agnes Pool

The *Four Tulips* or *Crossed Tulips* quilt is a variation of a pattern published in the <u>Ladies Art Company</u>: number 453. The tulip bloom is the same although where the stems crossed, Natie added a contrasting yellow block. The fabric for the small yellow squares was used in the first quilt shown, *Robbing Peter to Pay Paul*, 35 years earlier.

Four Tulips Circa 1960 Owner: nephew, Jack Moore

Detail of Square

The dimensions are 84 x 84 inches, perfectly square as are the 16 inch blocks. Needle Turned Applique was used to attach the tulips to the background fabric. The purple frame and the pink slashing fabrics have not been noted in the documented quilts so far. These vividly colored tulips on print backgrounds were not made by a timid quiltmaker.

I have found another quilt that was made from this pattern. Natie and Mildred pieced one for niece, Dean Benson, when they pieced this one. The pink and purple fabrics came from her stash.

Aptly named *A Path to Piece*, a 1960s pattern, this quilt had been folded away since Natie quilted it. One can only suppose that she made this one to be used in the nursing home when needed.

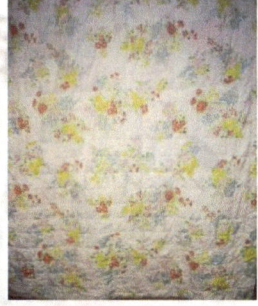

Path to Piece   72″ x 80″   Circa 1965
Owner: nephew, Marvin E. Carden

The quilting pattern is a 3 inch grid as shown on the whole cloth printed back. The back is turned to front as a binding. The 13″ blocks are set together with a large print that has purple and blue flowers, not a documented fabric.

This **Fan Doll** is a variation of *Sun Bonnet Sue,* a pattern made famous by Marie Webster in the early 1900s, and the earlier *Fanny's Fan* pattern.

The light blues in the sashing with the dark blue blocks made great frames for the appliqued and embroidered Fan Dolls. Notice that the skirts (fan blades) are different, possibly some left over from *Dresden Plate* blocks.

Owner: Great-niece, Ann Klecak

The decorative stitch used to applique these quilts was the Buttonhole or Blanket Stitch. Natie used six strands of embroidery floss when applying this technique.

Pretty *Butterflies* completed by 1975, twenty 12 inch squares make up this traditional appliqued pattern by Boag from 1935. Bright colors, especially orange and green, were very popular in the 1970s.

Butterflies 64" x 80"   Circa 1975 Owner: nephew, Tom Moore

The detailing on the butterflies shows well in these photos. Natie enjoyed making the black French Knots for the eyes. The parallel line quilting was in the sashing, with outline and diagonal in the squares.

This ***Strip Star*** variation of the *Spider Web Star* was made for J P, the brother in a nursing home. Not as well used as the earlier *Hour Glass* scrap quilt. The purple background fabric was the border on the earlier quilt made for him. The red plaid background was found in the *Caesar's Crown* quilt made over 25 years before this quilt. Newspaper was used for the paper piecing method to make these *Lemoyne Star* sections. This practice was the norm for strip quilts and date from the years after 1880 to 1980s for this quilt.

66" x" 82"   Circa 1980, Owner: sister, Mildred Pettus

The squares, 17 x 17 inch, were set together with a 4" multi stripe with contrasting pink 4" blocks in the sashing and zigzag quilting lines. The stars are quilted in the ditch.

Stitched on the back of this quilt.

This quilt is a pieced ***Tree of Life*** variation. Twenty 12 inch green and white squares set together with 3 inch print sashing and a 4 inch border was one of the most traditional quilts made by Natie. The seamed floral fabric used for the back is turned to the front as a binding.

Tree of Life 68" x 78" Circa 1980
Owner: nephew, Marvin E. Carden

In researching the variations of pieced tree patterns it was found that the traditional were all set in this manner. More recent patterns show them set on point.

Juzan is stitched on the back. This quilt has a few age spots! Maybe from pricked fingers?

This ***Grandmother's Flower Garden*** quilt has several areas of serious damage and needs restoration. Made of 3 inch hex pieces set in a mosaic pattern, the dimensions are 90" x 100".

Circa 1980   Owner: niece, Earlene Moore

The hex squares are exact.
The quilting was done in an outline stitch.

These blue fabrics were used in the *Fan Doll*.
There are two other quilts of this pattern.
One quilted by Natie but pieced by Mildred.

Made in 1988 by Natie, one of the last quilts she pieced, this ***Grandmother's Flower Garden*** is a true example of the talents of a seasoned hand quilter. The hex pieces fit exactly and are bordered in white to show them off. Another scrap quilt from her unlimited bag, although this one has a solid light peach colored whole cloth back and polyester batting.

Grandmother's Flower Garden   84" x 92"
Owner: Nephew, Johnny Moore

Signed and Dated

Natie's quilting frames, inherited from her mother, were wooden frames suspended from the ceiling. My mother has them now. Patterns were shared with family members, and with neighbors by cutting the shapes of the pieces from newspaper pages. Making an extra square and saving it as a pattern was a clever way to ensure that the techniques were preserved as well as fabric and color selection. Several newspaper pattern pieces and pieced pattern squares of vintage fabric have been preserved.

1983 newspaper for paper piecing the *Spider Web Star* quilt.

Dresden Plate Pattern Square. Fabrics are from *Four Tulips*

This *Maple Leaf* with an appliqued stem pattern square has a rusty pin securing the pattern pieces to the square.

Fan Doll pattern square.

Although not one of the quilt patterns documented, This is an interesting square with vintage fabrics. *Six Point Hex Star*, 1922 Ladies Art Company

This quilt was pieced in 1937 by one of her younger sisters, Mildred Juzan. Natie **quilted** this quilt by 1945. This one called *Southern Bell* is a variation of the *Colonial Lady* pattern by the Grandma Dexter Line, which was a very popular early 1930s pattern.

Southern Bell 68" x 88" Owner: sister, Mildred Pettus

The fabric for the quilt was purchased from the Company Store of the Shelby Iron Works by Mildred Juzan. Some of these fabrics, especially the plaids, were used in several of the later quilts made by Natie.

Mildred was 17 years old when she pieced the quilt top. She will be 93 in October, 2013. Natie was 28 when she quilted this one.

Path Through the Woods Circa 1945 66″ x 84″ Owner: sister, Mildred Pettus
Natie **quilted** this quilt that Mildred made from blue scraps.

Detail of Square

Feed Sacks on the back!

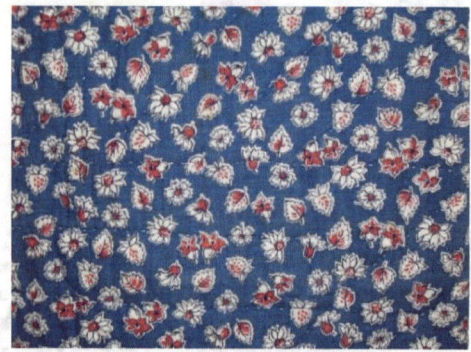

1945
Friendship Wreath
72" x 78"

Pieced in 1945 by Mildred, from a Lockport Batting pattern that was **quilted by Natie** that same year. The borders were made from an interesting lamp shade print. The close-up below shows the many small pieces necessary for one square (total of 42 of these) on the quilt. The solid green backing shows the parallel lines quilting pattern.

Owner: sister, Mildred Pettus

Belle Marie, the youngest sister, pieced this quilt of large scrap strips in an *Around the Block* pattern variation before 1950. The quilt was well used and well washed. The green stripe fabric near the top, and the gray fabric near the bottom right have worn through, and the cotton batting is showing. The rest of that green stripe fabric became the base of the *Grandmother's Fan* that Natie made in 1960. Notice the strip of blue on the right top; feed sacks from the *Path Through the Woods* that Mildred pieced in 1945.

The backing material is whole cloth print **quilted by Natie** in parallel lines**.**

Dimensions: 68″ x 86″

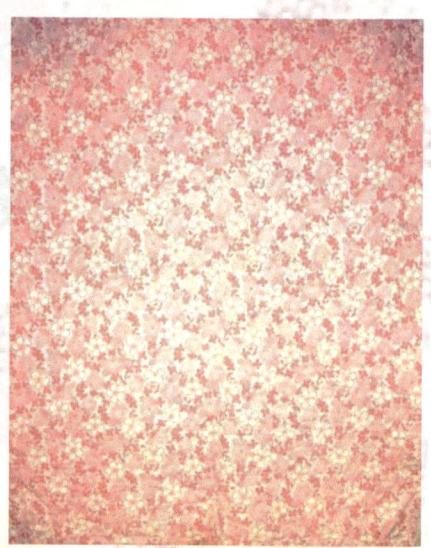

Owner: nephew, Marvin E. Carden

Natie **quilted** this *Grandmother's Fan* quilt for her sister Mildred, who pieced the quilt top in 1962. Size 68" x 88" The layout on this quilt was done in the opposite direction from the one that Natie pieced and quilted in 1960. One hundred and eight 6 inch squares were set so that the color placement was on the diagonal.

The fan patterns researched were set as the squares in this quilt.

Detail of fan blades.

Owner: nephew, Richard N. Carden

Backing: white muslin
Quilting: **Natie's** parallel lines!

Grandmother's Flower Garden   1987   72" x 84"
Pieced by Mildred Pettus and **quilted** by Natie Juzan
The border fabric was in the *Bars Quilt* from the 1950s.
This is the first of the documented quilts made with polyester batting.

Detail

Owner: sister, Mildred Pettus

Quilted by the piece, outline stitch and hemmed by machine.

Appliqued Rose

Appliqued Rose   1990   80" x 88"   Owner: sister, Mildred Pettus

In 1990, Natie **quilted** this *Rose Quilt* that Mildred appliqued and pieced. She did outline quilting in the squares and piano keys in the borders on this *Rose Quilt*, the last quilt she quilted. Her eyesight was getting bad and she had arthritis. She had worked with a ruler, scissors, thimble, needle and thread for the majority of her life.

She never married. She had no children. Ah, but what a legacy she left! She made quilts because they were needed. She made quilted treasures while she was making do!

***Robbing Peter to Pay Paul* August 2012**

Machine pieced and machine appliqued by Agnes M. Pool.
Long arm machine quilted by Lura Campell

Instructions for Robbing Peter to Pay Paul Quilt

Robbing Peter to Pay Paul **Quilt**   66" x 82"

Fabrics

4 Yards Brown Print (One way design does not work well with this pattern)
2 Yards Blue Print
1 Yard   Brown Textured
5 Yards Backing
81" x 90" Batting

Cutting

From Brown Print	Cut 48 Squares 9 ½" x 9 ½"
From Blue Print	Cut 164 of Pattern A, Press under 3/8"
	Cut 28 of Pattern B, Press under 3/8"
	Cut 7 Strips 2 ½' x WOF for Binding
From Brown Textured	Cut 6 Strips 5" x WOF for Border

Assembly -- Machine Applique

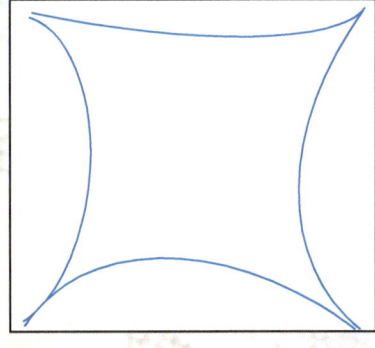

1. Applique Pattern A to all 4 sides of 24 of the 9 ½" Squares for inner squares of 2 through 4 for 6 rows.
2. Applique Pattern A to 3 sides of 20 of the 9 ½" Squares for top, bottom and both side rows.
3. Applique Pattern A to 2 sides of 4 of the 9 ½" Squares for corners of first and last row.

Press and sew 6 squares to make each row following outline.

Sew together to make 8 rows. Press seams open.

9 ½" Square

Sew side borders, then top and bottom to quilt top. Press seams open.

Align center of each Pattern B with border/quilt seams; applique to border and quilt top.

Layer and Quilt

Sew Binding strips together. Sew to front of quilt; turn to back and hem.

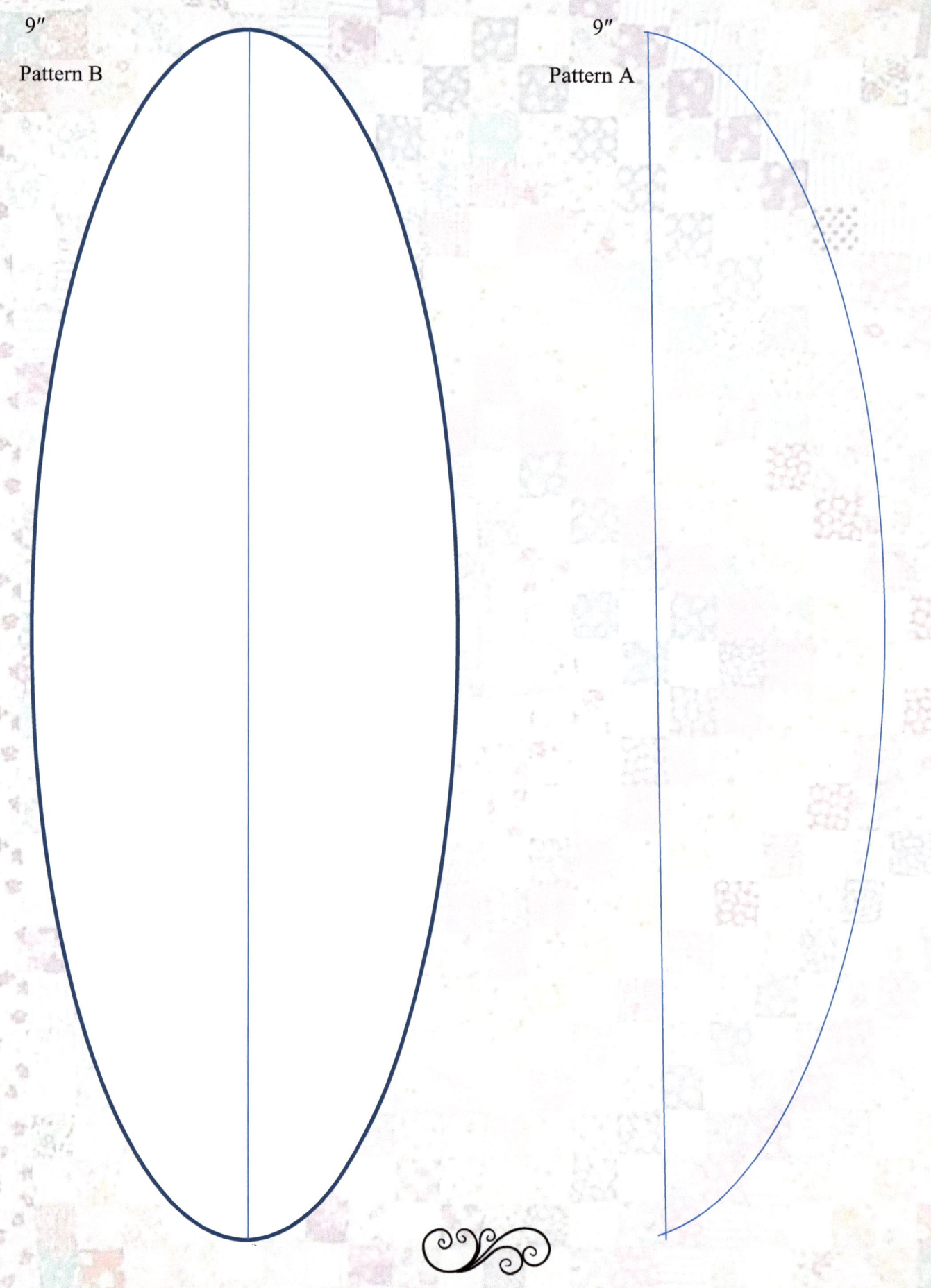

Trip Around the World Lap Quilt 53" x 62"
September 2012 Machine pieced by Agnes M. Pool, and hand quilted by Sarah Atchison.

Instructions for *Trip Around the World* Lap Quilt

Fabric Requirements
½ Yard each of Six Coordinating Fabrics
1/3 Yard of Matching Fabric for Inner Border
¾ Yard of Coordinating Fabric for Outside Border
1/3 Yard of Contrasting Fabric for Binding
60″ x 64″ Backing and Batting

Cutting
Cut Three 3 ½″ Strips WOF of each of the Six Fabrics
Cut 5   2″ Strips WOF for Inner Border
Cut 5   5″ Strips WOF for Outside Border
Cut 5   2 ½″ Strips WOF for Binding

Sewing
Arrange Strips in pleasing order—Light to Dark or Dark to Light

Sew the strips right sides together using a scant quarter inch seam-three sets of six strips each.

Press the seams in alternate directions. Sew first strip to last strip making a tube of the six fabrics. Do this on each set of strips.

With a rotary cutter, cut 3 ½″ strips from the sewn tubes. Cut 36 Strips.

Carefully pick out the stitches in each ring to make a strip of colors. Open the first ring at the first color, so the squares are in the order of 1, 2, 3, 4, 5, 6. Open the next row of the ring to the second square making it the top of that strip. Do this until the sixth row is the reverse of row 1. Sew the first strip to second strip, second to third and so on until 6 strips are sewn. Sew **one** more strip to this section for the center strip, making sure the order of the squares is correct. This makes the ″ up″ part of the left top of the quilt. Repeat these steps to make six strips for the right top of the quilt. Turn the right part top to bottom to make the right part of the top of the quilt (down part of the quilt) – a mirror image of the left side. Sew to the center strip to make the top of the quilt, making 13 rows of strips.

Press the seams from the outside to the center. Half of the quilt is done!

Repeat this process exactly the same. Now you have two halves.

You will notice the center rows are the same. Use two rings opened out to make the center to complete the design, adding a 3 ½″ square of the correct color to complete the design. Stitch the halves together.

Press the center row with the seam allowance toward the center.

Sew three more rows, keeping with the color placement, to add to the bottom to make the quilt longer. Press the quilt top.

Sew 2″ Border, sides first, then top and bottom to quilt top. Press toward border.

Sew 5″ Border in same manner. Press toward second Border.

Layer and Quilt.

Sew Binding Strips together. Fold in half and Press. Sew to front of quilt. Turn to back and Hem. Sew Label on Back.

Chapter Three

Gathering and Hanging the Quilts

Because the legacy quilts were in family member's possession, gathering and collecting them became the first priority. This documentation project was made possible with the assistance of those family members. Forms and the cost of quilt stands and photographing the quilts were money issues, other than the traveling and time spent transporting them.

The first four quilts came from Laurel Hill and Pensacola, Florida. Our first trial and error photography session gave us several photographs that we could use and several that we could not as the lighting was not the best. Tip: Outside lighting is best and some garages are not air conditioned.

Four of the quilts came from Talladega County, Alabama. These were some of the older quilts and some of the last quilts. Some of these photos were taken with the quilts hanging vertically and some on the floor.

The next seven documented and photographed came from West Blockton, Alabama. We photographed them in the garage with the not-so-perfect lighting. As we were not sure about several of them, we did not get photos of all that were brought. Again, my garage was not cool.

My sister helped me with four of the quilts from my family. We documented those at her house and one at my home. She and her husband held them up while I used my digital camera to photograph them.

It was not until all the forms and photos were assembled and placed in a portfolio, and the comparisons begun, that I realized more information was needed to complete all the data for an accurate documentation. Several decades of the quilts were incomplete. Searching for her quilts began anew. We knew there were questions about several of the quilts from West Alabama. Those were brought again. Two more were added to the documentation.

Our aunt from Talladega County came up with three more that were packed away. This brought the total documented to 25. There are four quilts still out there. One is too fragile to handle. The locations of the other three are known, but unfortunately have not been documented.

It was also decided that there had to be a better way to hang the quilts to photograph them. As there is a planned exhibit, quilt hangers will be needed for that part of this project. There are several kinds of quilt hangers. After much research on the different kinds, two were purchased. One is the type that is balanced from the center; the other is on a tripod. Both require using Hanging Sleeves.

Making a Hanging Sleeve

From Wide Muslin cut a strip 9″ by the width of the quilt.

Fold under short edges ¼″, wrong sides together. Fold under again and press. Stitch down.

Fold lengthwise, wrong sides together. Sew with a ½″ seam. Press open.

Place open seam to quilt back. Center and pin top edge to the back of the quilt ½″ below the binding. Whip stitch the top edge to the quilt back.

Make a ½″ fold along the length of the sleeve to create a pleat. Pin the sleeve bottom to the quilt.

Whip stitch the lower edge of the sleeve to the quilt. Remove pins.

Hang quilt on rod/tripod type hanger or from dowel type.

For use on the balanced type hanger, measure from side to center and make two sleeves to allow for center bracket.

Sewing the sleeve on the back of the Dresden Plate quilt that belongs to me made hanging the quilt so much easier. Sewing the sleeve can be permanent or temporary. As mine will be displayed, the sleeve will stay on.

Butterfly Baby Quilt   40″ x 48″

Machine appliqued and pieced by Agnes M. Pool and hand quilted by Sarah Atchison, this ***Butterfly Baby Quilt*** is a scaled-down version of the ***Butterfly*** quilt made in 1975.

Instructions for the *Butterfly Baby Quilt*

Fabric Requirements Based on 40" Width

- 2 ½ Yards White Muslin for Background and Backing
- 1 Yard   Pink Print for Butterfly Wings and Sashing
- ½ Yard   Light Purple for Border
- 1/3 Yard Pink for Binding
- Scraps of Assorted Pink, Purple and Green Solids for Butterfly Body
- 2 Skeins of Dark Green Embroidery Thread

Cutting

- Cut 12   10 ½" Squares of White Muslin
- Cut 12   A for Butterflies from Pink Print
- Cut 12   B from Solid Scraps
- Cut 8   1 ½" Strips WOF from Pink Print
  - Cut 8 1 ½" x 10 ½" Strips for sashing between the inner squares
  - Cut 5 1 ½" x 33" Strips for sashing between the rows
  - Cut 2 1 ½" x 46" for Side Strips
- Cut 4   3 ½" Strips WOF from Light Purple for Border
- Cut 5   2 ½" Strips WOF from Pink for Binding

Sewing

Fold Muslin Squares in half and then fold again to find centers. Pin Butterfly Wings to Squares at an angle as if in flight. (For Raw Edge Applique: apply fusible to fabric before cutting A and B and machine applique them to squares.)

Applique Butterfly Wings to Muslin Squares. Applique Butterfly Bodies to Butterfly. Do Outline Stitch Embroidery to make antenna and body seams. Eyes are French Knots.

Lay Quilt Squares out to position Butterflies. Sew 1 ½" x 10 ½" slashing to inside squares.

Sew 1 ½" x 33" slashing to top and bottom of the first row and then to second row. Continue until all four rows are together ending with slashing on bottom of the last row.

Sew 1 ½" x 46" to left and right sides.

Sew Light Purple Border to the sides then top and bottom.

Layer and Quilt.

Sew Binding Strips together, Fold in half and Press. Sew to quilt, turn to back and hem.

Sew label on the quilt back.

Add 3/8" for turning under for applique

Butterfly Body

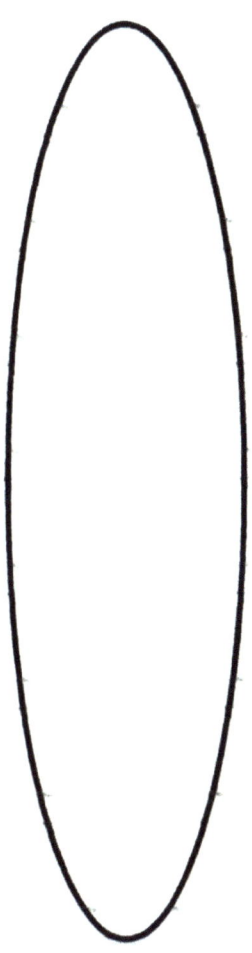

Add 3/8" for applique

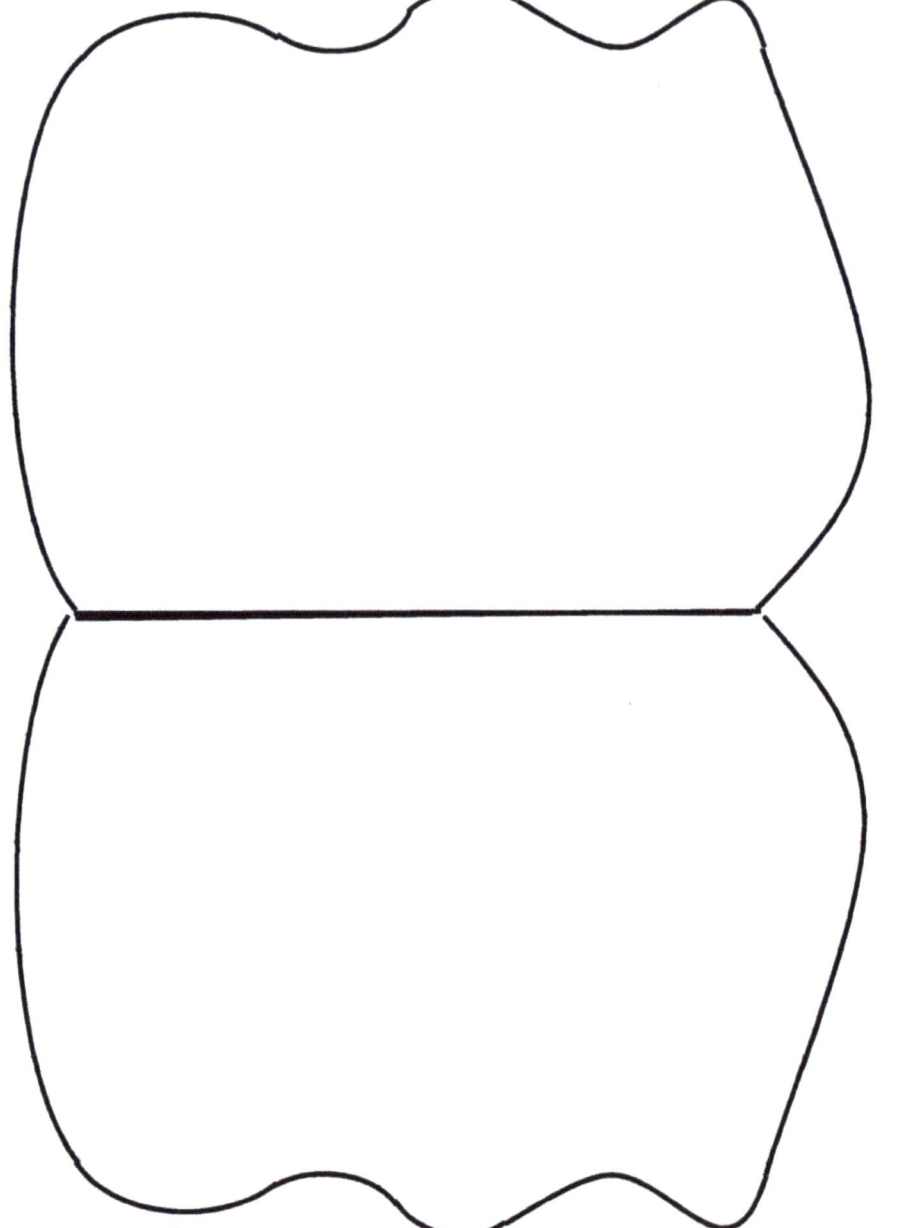

Butterfly Wings

Dresden Plate **Table Runner**

20″ x 56″ Inspired by the *Dresden Plate* quilt made by Lillian Natie Juzan. Adapted from a Virginia Robertson design, the table runner is hand appliqued, machine pieced and machine quilted by Agnes M. Pool, June 2012.

Instructions for making the *Dresden Plate* Table Runner

Fabrics   Based on 40" width

1 Yard Cream Textured

½ Yard Green plus 3 Fat Quarters of Assorted Greens

½ Yard Red Print

1 Fat Quarter - Gold

24 X 60 for Backing and Batting

Cutting

From Cream	Cut 3	12" Squares for applique background.
	Cut 4	8" Squares—Cut diagonally for 8 half square triangles.
From Green	Cut 1	4 ½" Strip WOF. Using Pattern Cut 42 sections for Dresden Plates
	Cut 1	4" Strip WOF
	Cut 2	2 ½" WOF to make 104" for Binding
From Gold	Cut 2	4 ½' Strips from Fat Quarter
From Red Print	Cut 4	1 3/4" WOF for Borders
	Cut 3	3" Circles for centers of Dresden Plates

Piecing

Fold Dresden Plate sections together, stitch across, turn and press. Sew 14 sections together and applique to background square. Make three. Baste ¼ inch around Red Print Circles and turn to make centers. Applique to plate centers. Square to 11".

Sew Red Print Borders to Squares.

Sew Gold 4 ½" Strips together, sew Gold and Green Strips together lengthwise. Press and cut into 4 ½" rectangles. Sew to make four patch squares. Make 4 total. Sew to Cream Half Square Triangles for a total of four setting sections.

Assemble according to diagram/photo.

Layer and Quilt.   Sew Label to back.

Dresden Plate Table Runner   20" x 56"

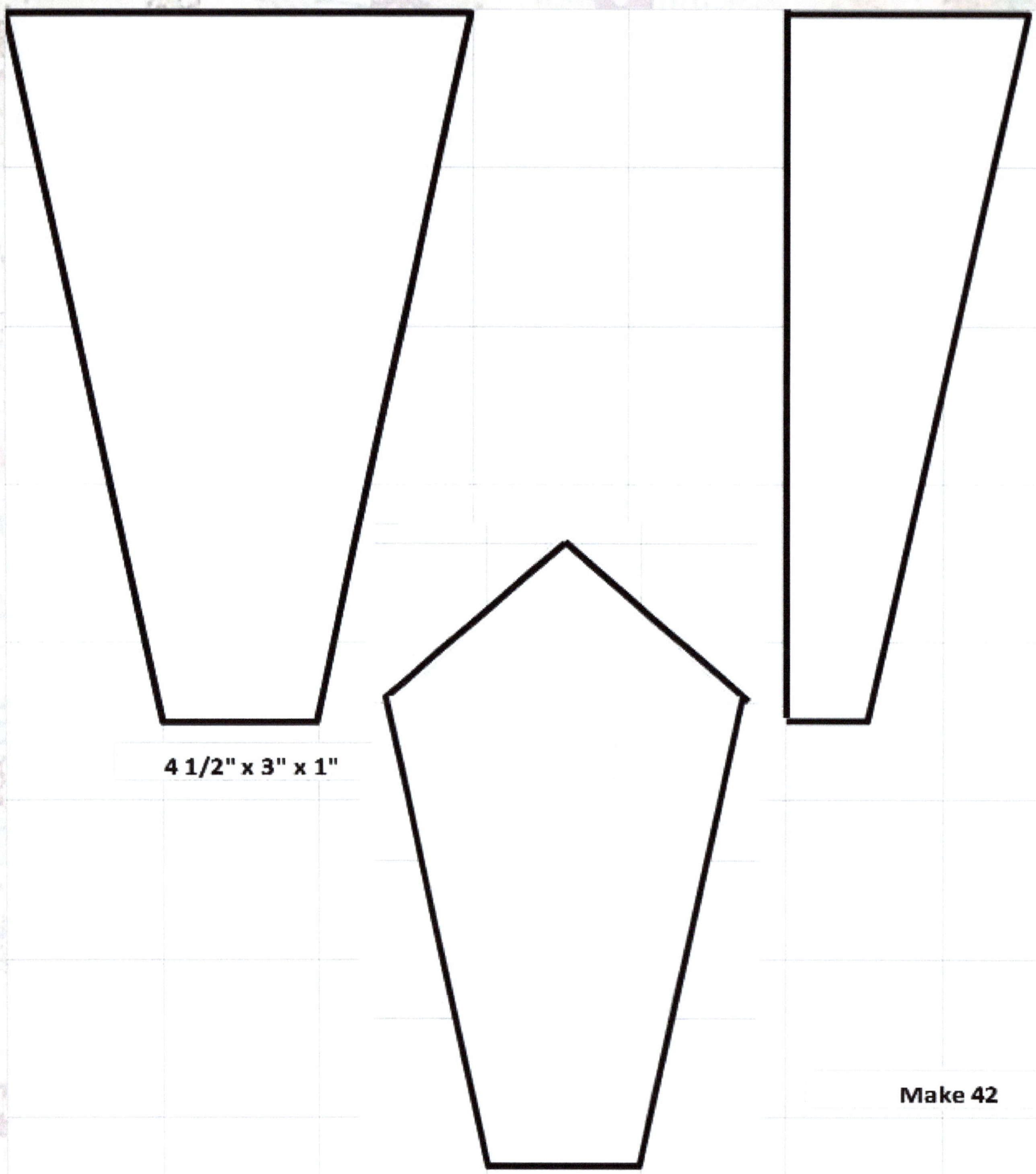

4 1/2" x 3" x 1"

Make 42

Chapter Four

PLANNING AN EXHIBITION

Due to the fact that most of the original yards of fabrics purchased were from retailers in Shelby County and the fact that Shelby County was the home of my family, I felt that a first showing of these quilts should be local. I immediately set out to find a venue with a date to display and exhibit the quilts.

Some of the fabrics in several of the documented quilts from the 1930s and 1940s were purchased from the Company Store of the Shelby Iron Works in Shelby, Alabama. The Juzan family lived two miles west of the store and frequently purchased items from the facility. As the oldest son worked for the Iron Company and was paid in tokens that could only be redeemed at the store, a common practice at a company store, the family traded there. The Iron Works Company Store closed by the early 1950s and the building later destroyed. The property has since become The Shelby Iron Works Museum and Park.

The " Company Store"

As part of the rebuilding of Shelby Iron Works which began in 1868, a new commissary soon took its place among the other substantial and impressive brick buildings. Upon its completion, the " company store" was opened not only to iron company employees and their families, but also to the entire community. This was done by the company to help relieve the destitute condition following the Civil War. The commissary had a basement and adjacent warehouse. A portion of the warehouse can be seen on far right of the photo. Standing in front are Shelby Iron employees who staffed the commissary.

Permission by Shelby Iron Works Association.

From Clothing to Hardware and More

Constructed during the rebuilding of 1868-1870, the large three story brick building, situated across from the New Dannemora Hotel, soon became the commissary to the community of Shelby.
The well stocked store offered everything from clothing, to hardware, to coffins.
This building contained, in addition to the store, iron company offices and a basement laboratory. A large warehouse was located behind the commissary building.
During the late 1800's and early 1900's Shelby was a booming town and saw the addition of a number of other stores offering a wide variety of goods and services.

Permission of the Shelby Iron Works Association

Linen scarf purchased in 1940 at the Company Store by John Juzan for Mildred Juzan.

I contacted the officials at the Iron Works Park about available space on the facility for an exhibit of vintage quilts. They were very receptive when they heard that some of the fabrics used to make the vintage quilts were purchased from the Commissary at the Shelby Iron Works in the 1930s and 1940s. The exhibit was in one of the newer, smaller buildings on the grounds during the Fall Festival in October 2012. See photos.

Getting the word out about the Exhibit was the next focus in the process. Several flyers were made and distributed in the area. The officials of the Park allowed the flyers to be included with their displays advertising the event.

The day before the exhibit was the set-up and workday. Remember now this is a not a commercial event! Getting all the quilts, the racks and stands and all the things to carry this showing off took two trips to the park. A friend brought his truck over and helped with transporting the larger items.

Since hanging a quilt exposes it to stress from hanging and lighting, a short-term exhibit from one to three days was the more practical duration of the exhibit; therefore the Fall Festival fits the time frame exactly. Also, since the quilts have both sentimental and high market value, it is important that the quilts be monitored while on display. The officials of the park were allowing me to have exclusive use of the building, so monitoring was my responsibility.

Care was taken with deciding on placement in the building so that when the quilts were displayed they would not have to be moved for the whole weekend. White gloves were worn to handle the quilts and to show the backs. Over 300 signed the guest registration. The children attending were allowed to put on gloves and touch the quilts as the different patterns and fabrics were pointed out to them.

There was a card with information about the history of the quilt. A guest registration table was available at the entrance to the exhibit. Photographs and biography of the quiltmaker were on this table along with a caution regarding touching the quilts on display.

Several of the quilts were displayed vertically using the purchased quilt hangers and rods, and utilizing the sewn quilt sleeves. Some of the older, more fragile quilts were folded and displayed on tables and smaller quilt racks. The quilts were attractively displayed in chronological and historical groupings throughout the room. Color and design groupings were considered and displayed when possible, but as the majority of these quilts are multi-colored scrap quilts, displaying according to hue was somewhat challenging. The two color-coordinated ones: the Tree of Life and the Appliqued Rose, were displayed together on one rack The photographer made photos of the quilts as they were being arranged and displayed. After they were arranged to her satisfaction, she photographed them in groups and according to the arrangement style.

Natie's quilts exhibited at Shelby Iron Works Park

Tree of Life Wall Hanging 32 ½″ x 32 ½″

July 2012 Machine pieced and quilted by Agnes M. Pool

This Tree of Life Wall Hanging was inspired by the quilt Natie made in 1980. The square is set on point, and an interesting border print was used for the outside border/frame.

Pattern and instructions for Tree of Life Block and Wall Hanging

Tree of Life Wall Hanging   32 ½" x 32 ½"

12 ½" Tree of Life pieced block layout

Fabrics

1 Yard Green Print

½ Yard Cream Tone on Tone

1 ½ Yards Border Print with 2 ½″ and 5″ Repeat

1 Yard Backing Fabric

36 X 36 Batting

Yardage based on 40″ wide.

Cutting

From Green   Cut 8   3 7/8″ Squares—Cut 7 in half diagonally to make 14 half square triangles –the eighth square will be base of the tree.
Cut 1   2 ¾″ Square for trunk of tree.
Cut 4   5″ WOF for Border
Cut 4   2 ½″ WOF for straight grain binding

From Cream   Cut 6   3 7/8″ Squares –Cut in 4 in half diagonally to make 8 half square triangles —the other two squares will be corners.
Cut 2   2 ¾″ x 5 ½″ rectangles for joining trunk to tree.
Cut 2   5 ½″ Squares –Cut in half diagonally to make half square triangles.

From Print   Cut 4   2 ½″ x 24″ Border Strips.
Cut 4   4 ½″ x 40″ Border Fabric

Construction

Sew Cream and Green Half Square Triangles to make 8 Squares.

Sew rows together according to diagram. Square to 12 ½ inches for on point setting.

Sew small border strips to cream half square triangles to make 9 ½″ corners. Sew triangles to 12 ½ inch square, mitering the corners. Square to 17 ½″.

Sew Green Border, mitering the corners. (30 inches finished to 25 inches)

Sew Print Border, mitering the corners. (38 finished to 32 ½ inches)

Layer and Quilt

Sew the binding strips. Press wrong sides together.

Sew to quilt front, turn to back and blind stitch to back.

Make label and sew on back.

My *Spider Web Strip Star* Wall Hanging   36″ x 36″

Inspired by *the Strip Star Quilt*, machine pieced and quilted by Agnes Pool, May 2012

The star pattern pieces were cut from the newspaper pattern for the foundation piecing.

1983 Newspaper
Pattern Pieces

Spider Web Strip Star

Block Size 17 inches Square

Cut 8 for Foundation

Paper Piecing Strip Star

Spider Web Strip Star Wall Hanging

Finished Size: 36″ x 36″

Fabric and Cutting Requirements

10 Fat Quarters of coordinating fabrics cut into random strips for Star sections and pieced Border -- or use scraps from your stash.

¼ Yard of Background fabric –From background fabric cut six 6″ squares for filling in the square. Four for corners and two cut in half on the diagonal for sides, top and bottom.

½ Yard of Contrasting fabric for Small Border and Binding –Cut 4 – 1 ½″ WOF for Border.

Then cut 5-2 ½″ WOF for Straight Binding.

½ Yard of Coordinating Print for outside border – Cut 4 -- 5″ WOF

1 ¼ Yard Backing fabric

Batting – 40″ x 40″

Yardage is based on 40″ wide.

Assembling the quilt

Sew random strips on foundation paper piecing star sections. Trim to pattern size. Sew sections alternately with background pieces until all sections form the square. Remove foundation pattern paper carefully and press completed square. Trim to 17″.

Scw assorted strips to make 4″ Pieced Borders. Sew border sides, then top and bottom, adjusting the strips as necessary.

Add 1 ½″ Border. Sew border sides, then top and bottom.

Add 5″ Border sides, then top and bottom.

Layer and Quilt as desired.

Join Binding strip diagonally. Fold binding in half lengthwise, wrong sides together, and press to make a fold. Sew binding to quilt front. Turn binding to the back and whipstitch to finish.

Sew label on back.

Chapter Five

Lessons Learned

The working title given to this assignment really tells exactly what I have learned from this journey regarding the legacy of my aunt's quilts. <u>Making Treasures While Making Do!</u> Quilts are treasures, whether still in the possession of the maker or cherished by family members or individuals who later acquire them.

Natie's quilts are aesthetic and emotionally pleasing to all who share in her legacy. Quilts are aesthetically pleasing through the placement of color: this I have learned. Aesthetics add value. Emotion, because she was family, was already involved.

She used many different patterns to construct her quilts. Of the 26 quilts documented, 21 different patterns were used. She was partial to the fan pattern, fond of embroidery and black embroidery thread, and she appliqued extremely well. She hand quilted in parallel lines.

Patterns of traditional quilts are not simple. They are involved, with intricate, small pieces that if not cut and sewn precisely, will not fit in a 7 x 7 or 12 inch square correctly. Applique consumes a lot of time and requires patience. Two more things I have learned: pattern and accurate construction add value.

There are many pattern names for traditional quilts. Regional names were used for some of the documented quilts. *Trip Around the World* is known in Alabama as *Around the Mountain*, and the *Colonial Lady* as the *Southern Bell* or the *Umbrella Girl*. Without the quilt history and pattern books on my shelves, this project would have been trashed at the beginning.   References for pattern identification are absolutely necessary for a documentation project.

How-to videos will not teach you to make a good photograph.   Save time; hire a professional to take the pictures of the quilts. All the racks, hangers, sleeves and accessories will not make a photo look good if the photographer is unskilled. I have proof of this; saved on the hard drive of my computer.

Showing quilts is a huge undertaking, and with no prior experience, absolutely daunting. Knowledgeable assistance would have been great. Studying and reading instructions on how to stage an exhibit is a little different than the actual showing of the quilts.

Attendance was better on the first day. The building was small and caused delays for guests in getting in to view the quilts. Cloudy with a chance of rain on the second day but favorable comments on the quilts and the displays made it all worthwhile.

Cousins Kay Moore, Brenda Moore from Florida, Marvin Carden from Westblockton in Alabama and my aunt Mildred Pettus, Sylacauga came to the Festival and to see what I had done with their quilts. My mom, Vonzelle Moore and my sister, Dean Benson also came down and checked things out.

My friends and co-workers from the Library, Shelia Gallups, Retta Authier, and Mary Young viewed the layout of things and gave me a high five. Three hundred plus visitors viewed the vintage quilts during the two day show.

This project has been a trial and error endeavor. The lessons learned are unforgettable ones, but freely shared. I have loved every minute of pursuing my assignment, including the messed up fabric that I am saving for another day, for some other project. Two of the quilt patterns I attempted did not turn out to be salvageable, but I have mastered foundation paper piecing.

In with the patterns saved, we found a Mountain Mist batting wrapper from 1940. The pattern on the inside is # 77, the *Palms* or *Hosanna*. I could not resist this one. A fitting grand finale for this awesome quilt documentation journey!

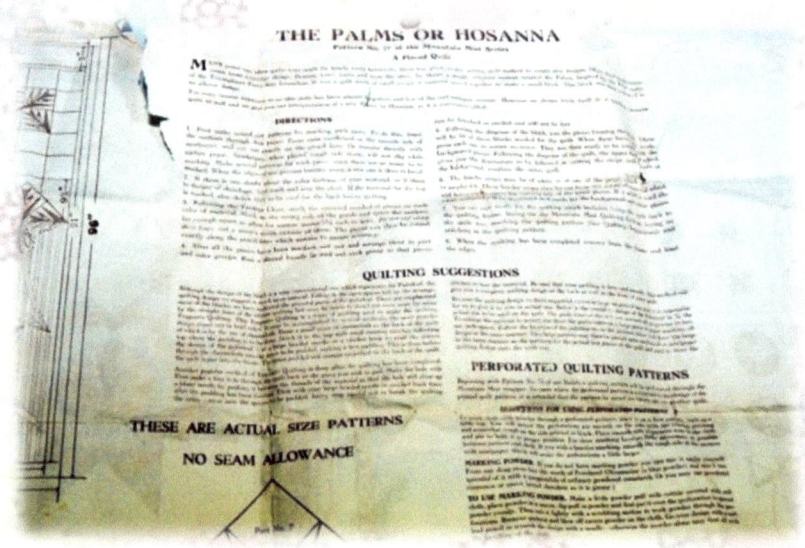

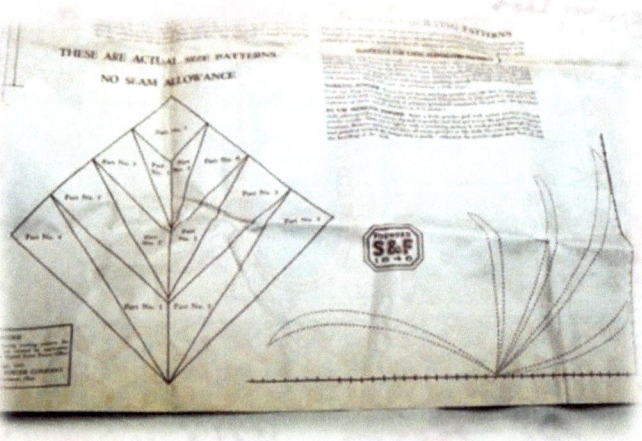

Hosanna in my frames for hand quilting. October 1, 2012

References

Boag, Chicago, Illinois 1927

Brackman, Barbara. *Encyclopedia of Applique.* C & T Publishing, Inc. P.O. Box 1456, Lafayette, CA 94549, 2009

Brackman, Barbara. *Encyclopedia of Pieced Patterns.* Paducah, KY 42002-3290: American Quilter's Society 1993

Dexter, Grandma. Virginia Snow Studios, Elgin Illinois. 1930

Finley, Ruth E. *Old Patchwork Quilts and The Women Who Made Them.* Philadelphia and London. JP. Lippincott, Company. 1929

Havig, Bettina. *Carrie Hall Blocks.* Paducah, KY, P.O. Box 3290, Paducah, KY. American Quilter's Society 1999

Ladies Art Company, *Quilt Pattern Book-Patchwork and Applique.* St. Louis, MO 1922

Lockport Batting Company, Lockport, NY

Mountain Mist, Steams & Foster, Cincinnati, Ohio, 1940

Shelby Iron Works Park and Museum, P. O. Box 176, Shelby, AL 35143

Virginia Robertson Designs, Dolores, CO, 81323

Webster, Marie D. *Quilts: Their Story and How to Make Them.* New York: Tudor Publishing, 1915

ABOUT THE AUTHOR

Agnes M. Pool has been quilting for almost 50 years. Quilting is in her blood. Her mother, aunts, both grandmothers and great grandmothers were quilters. She and her sisters were taught to quilt by her mother. She is both a hand quilter and machine quilter. She lectures, teaches workshops and is a quilt appraiser. She has written another book due to be published in 2014. She has one daughter and two grandchildren. She lives in Shelby County, Alabama with her dog, Sobe.

Notes

Notes